CW01391017

Terminarchy

Terminarchy

Angela France

Nine
Arches
Press

Terminarchy
Angela France

ISBN: 978-1-913437-17-6
eISBN: 978-1-913437-18-3

Copyright © Angela France.

Cover artwork © Fumio Obata. www.fumioobata.co.uk

All rights reserved. No part of this work may be reproduced, stored or transmitted in any form or by any means, graphic, electronic, recorded or mechanical, without the prior written permission of the publisher.

Angela France has asserted her right under Section 77 of the Copyright, Designs and Patents Act 1988 to be identified as the author of this work.

First published July 2021 by:

Nine Arches Press
Unit 14, Sir Frank Whittle Business Centre,
Great Central Way, Rugby.
CV21 3XH
United Kingdom

www.ninearchespress.com

Printed in the United Kingdom by:
Imprint Digital

Nine Arches Press is supported using public funding by Arts Council England.

Supported using public funding by
**ARTS COUNCIL
ENGLAND**

Contents

Poetry Makes Nothing Happen

W.H. Auden

Let it make nothing happen more, this year,
                        so that a young girl
whose mail arrives early can read the book she's waited for
over breakfast and find a poem with blue depths and points
of light which she tastes in the back of her throat on the way
to work and walks a little slower than usual so that nothing
happens as she crosses the road because the guy in the 4x4
who was answering a call on his mobile already passed by.

Or so that a fighter sits up almost all night reading Rumi, trying
to understand death and blood, peace and love and sleeps
too late to be ready for the knock at the door so tells them
he'll follow after because he wants to hold his son and play
with his daughter and nothing happens as he kisses his children
because he isn't in the car when a government missile hits it.

Or so that a man, sleepless and pacing, picks up a book
from his wife's bedside and reads a poem casually
but finds lines stuck in his mind like burrs on a wool sock
like when he used to spend weekends relaxed and outdoors
so that he holds back on giving an order and extends
credit on a couple of loans so that nothing happens
to a lot of people that day who carry on going to work
and never even know that nothing happened.

Threshold

Every house has something of a whale at its entrance.
Bleached vertebrae, their jutting transverses
arm-span wide, set at the wall's base
where long grass cords through their spaces,
perched on the stone post as if about to fly,
or carefully alcoved into the wall.

A scapula buttresses a wall, a jawbone curves
against stone, each whitened and cracked
in alien air, and a weathered pair of ribs arc
over a gate, lost promise of a heart-cage.

When the wind booms through the lane
and the sea bellows over rocks to bite the field-edge,
you could think the bones tremble and shift,
yearn together to take their old places. A spine, a shoulder,
the suggestion of a tail-fluke in the bending trees.

Water Mark

Water geysers from the road, tarmac humped
and cracked as if pushed up by tree roots over years.
It gushes muddily down the road, bubbles
over gutter-dams of twigs and leaves, splits on a bend
to follow the camber, denies the road its definition.

The woman at the water board's *Leak Line*
wants to know the name of the road.
It doesn't have one. I could tell her
how the road rises from the town,
leaving street names behind,
it is a road to somewhere or from
elsewhere, how it is a place between.

I could tell her how often I have followed
the road to climb the hill for consolation,
for exercise or delight.
I have managed its bends, driving in a hurry
or not, know how the land drops away
from the road edge, looks over
the flickering clutter of town at night.

She says she can't send a crew without a postcode.
I could tell her I know that old sycamore, leaning
over a crumbling wall, how this bend tightens
if you come down the hill too fast. There are houses
backing into the hillside, hidden behind trees
and shrubs, stately gateposts by the road
with blurred names carved
into lichened stone, no numbers.

I tell her they can follow the water, track
up the streams from where the road leads
into town, past street names and houses
with postcodes. The water knows where it is.

What Remains

A sudden absence over the field,
a flicker of space, a silence
and the swifts are gone.
Their dark nests under the eaves
wait, gather cobwebs, dust, leaves
tossed from high trees. It is hard
to remember how they return,
carrying light on their wingtips.

Some things remain. A low sun
through a scribble of bare trees,
the robin defending his space
over tree, hedge, and bird table.
Hips and haws scatter jewels
in leafless briars and the sparrows
strut, carouse, squabble and shrug
their wide-boy shoulders,
know this is their manor, all year.

Early Spring

Under a March sun, the bank by the old wall blooms
springtime. Bluebells nod, celandine and primrose lift faces
and whitethorn canopies over the top in imitation of stars
reflected by saxifrage below. Sparrow moans at my shoulder
No, too soon! Too soon!

Ferns spread like opening hands, leaf-tips curled ammonite-tight,
tender spikes of new grass stand up from yellowed clumps,
there's enough warmth in the air for bare arms, and at home
the heating's been off for weeks. Sparrow mutters behind me
We'll pay for this!

On the news, there are flooded towns and villages,
rescues from storm-rushed homes, small islands of livestock
in sodden fields. A video online of another ice-shelf calving
and a neighbour walks by, calling out 'lovely day!'
Mark my word, we'll pay for this.

Stone-glow

I would see in the dark if I could
  channel stone-light through my feet
  granite's smoky glow
     the changing shades of sandstone
  but the roads and carparks weep
        fake rainbows to block pores
  and baffle sound
The trees know there is still light
they can draw through vein and branch
    which strengthens roots to crack
       and lift paving slabs
they talk in stone-words under earth
    to whisper of breath and survival
and they know
       we can't see in the dark

After

When they came out, blinking in the summer light
noise swelled in the streets. Shouts from neighbours
they'd forgotten, unfamiliar traffic, a roar from planes
stitching the clouds. Shop-shutters rattle while queues
elbow-jab and jostle, markets unveil their tarpaulins,
pile their goods. Pavements and roads filled with people
shaking hands, hugging. Some stood still counting
the gaps and some waited in doorways and gates
with nowhere to go.
                            Some burst out of doors
stretching their mouths and fingers, grasping everything
in reach, cramming clothes, shoes, toiletries, past teeth
and tongues. They crowd roads, tangle the traffic
to gridlock, swarm over roofs, break windows, tear tyres
with their teeth. They storm into stores, clear the shelves,
eat baskets, fittings, tills, stagger through doors, still hungry.
                            Some watch from their doorsteps,
step back inside, close their doors, pull down their blinds.

We know the Wantwite

born from shells and stones and the hides of
beasts sucking silver   gold   from the earth
to fill its veins   whining through slimy
teeth   crying for *more, more*   Greed-grown
fungal-toed   feet   slapping   careless
crushing new shoots   small gods   wishes

Small Gods

Our gods are poor things, these days,
bereft of altars, priests, or homes,
worshipped through clicks and clichés
and starved though we try to atone
through getting and losing, the sacrifice
of things we don't need. We've grown
past thunder and threat, gods in disguise
to walk among us as man or bull; strength
only known or used as a way to victimise
different thoughts or ways to enhance
helpless lives. We've lost Thor's hammer
Apollo's bow and Odin's mead, take offence
at any prick to our comfort while we clamour
on keyboards for anything to fill the holes
they've left. We may edit a page's banner
to signal who we are but try to control
anything real, of blood and flesh,
by pinning to screens where we can scroll
past whatever disturbs. Copy, paste, refresh,
we are a worn people whose shrivelled gods
are enshrined in phone lenses as we try to possess
any thing to salve a communal sense of loss.

City Break

In this city, every face looks
like someone I've seen before.
I startle at the arch of a brow,
the plane of a cheek, double-take
at the shape a mouth makes in speaking.

My do-I-know-you half smile
has no currency here. I taste rust,
feel the grind and creak of locks seizing.
I am the knave in the king's court,
the stiff-jointed puppet on a dancer's stage.

Iron spreads through the roads,
grumbles in the drains, tricks my feet
into trips and skids as I brace
against the earth's spin; faster here
but with a stutter of hesitation,
a limp and hobble of a long-distance
runner nearing exhaustion

Growth

Cow parsley, mallow, and campion
narrow the path. Blackthorn chokes
the stile, spatters petals on the ground
like leucocytes.
        Everything blooms in May,
everything grows. I could bury my face
in the white and purple froth of flowers
at the field's edge, walk through thigh-high
stems damp with cuckoo-spit and dew,
watch the bees gorge on comfrey.
        I could sink into the scent,
lie below high umbels while chiff-chaffs call
from a scribble of young willows
but a mild winter forced blooms too soon,
too soon, and the bluebells are over;
only a shrivel of blue on show.
        At ground level, brown leaves droop,
meld into mulch, green stems drive
upwards. Ground elder and creeping thistle
rampage under the canopy, their roots
spearing through the soil. I can almost
hear them, like cells drumming through
the earth's veins.

Sparrow Complains

I thought I'd no time or space for him
between the keyboards and screens,
the rush of need and get, of demands
and should and musts.
            But here he is again,
speaking limestone with golden grains
under his tongue, quartz-sharp eyes
finding the cracks, the little places
where levering his ash thumbstick
could open a field gate, a hilltop, a wood.
He hobnails a counterpoint to keystrokes,
tilts winter sun off a wet holly leaf
to glare on screens, whispers wind
in dry leaves to my ear.
He grumbles along the street,
in my doorway, over my desk,
no room, he growls, *no room.*

On Balance

Starlings measure consistent distance
above and below, before and behind
to sweep and spiral in the evening sky.

At the edges they only see the dark
of starling and the light of sky,
balancing between them, a fulcrum
to shape the dance.

There is a space between light and shade,
a pivot to balance the time
when hedges darken to shadow
and streetlights slow-wake from daytime
drab; the time when curtains draw
to blind windows and roads quieten.

There is a shape to the time
when sparrows chunter to roost
and small creatures whisker their holes'
openings to taste the coming night.
The fulcrum's point is too fine
for clumsy feet; I stumble

in trying to hold the balance
between dark and light,
between caution and courage;
in trying to form the contour
between word and silence.

Scrolling

Carefully, I sort recycling on my knees
each bottle-chink in the bag, or silence
of plastic in the box feels like a plea,
a prayer.
        The crowd's insistence
on guilty clicks on *sad* or *angry* faces
dilutes the true significance
of the scrolling pictures, the glacial
cracks and calvings, rainforest fires,
storms and floods.
                Endless pages
of drowning refugees, tired
rescuers carrying bloodied babies
from bombed houses, scared
children sleeping rough in rich cities.
Scrolling feels like vertigo; hearts
and kittens don't dilute constant crises
and paying attention is like the stark
brilliance of winter sun on a wet road;
all I see ahead is the shape of something dark.

Wantwite gets clever

gather-grabs fine silks   brocades   spins
lengths   nets swathes folds around its
body   huge as a continent bedecks itself
sparkly in jewels and gems   coats its teeth
with pearls   softens growls to purrs learns
to smile   it squats over cities   leans over
towns   breaks down   hedges and hills
around villages   salts the earth

Junk

After 'Junk' by Richard Wilbur

The brook burbles its way   down over boulders

and gushes against   great rocks to cascade

and splash into the still   pool where spray

benefits a low bank   of bluebells and cowslips.

It is picture-book pretty,   a place to appreciate

our gorgeous earth,   to be grounded and grateful.

But Sparrow's at my shoulder   saying *look below,*

between molecules of clear water   are minute beads we make

of plastic and petroleum   and I know that under pebbles

and sand will be cellophane   and shattered picnic

plates, crisp packets   and playthings left behind

or discarded; if it drops   to the depth of diamonds

the hardening heat   won't help, won't heal,

there'll be no gems,   no glitter from this garbage.

Landlocked

I can hear no water-voices where I live.
The susurrus of a calm sea is miles away
and the river's splash and nibble
against the bank where I sometimes played
doesn't pass through this town.
There's no brook to chatter beside me
where I walk, only a still dew-pond
which dries to a grassy dip and fills
to a mirror where tips of grass-leaves
wave through the water's edge.

The garden is cushioned underfoot
with moss. By the roadside,
the verges sprout dandelions and daisies.
The land knows the water runs beneath,
out of earshot, talking to itself.

For a Glacier

For three days, hold cubes of ice in your mouth.
Don't suck or crunch, only replace them as they melt

to moisture. Dress only in white or lightest blue,
practice stillness, stasis, until the named day

when we will move slowly, stately, to the place.
Chant softly, steadily, different words of cold

from every language in the world while acolytes watch
the edge, sound their gongs for each slow drip.

Hold the rhythm, do not let it speed, hold the ice.

Singing lessons

I have tried to learn bird songs. I know the robin,
crying *mine! mine!* from cold branches.
I see his chest-puff and open throat through winter,
watch his notes boast through the air.
Blackbird sometimes shows himself, lets me watch
song spill from his beak, the liquid trill of his courting,
the sharp *chook chook* as he warns of a dog, or a cat,
or me. I know the jay, his hustling yawp and blue flash,
and a hedge-full of sparrows' chatter brightens my walk.

All the birds I don't know sing on spring mornings
from branches veiled in new leaves. I walk with binoculars
but can't match the whistles, warbles, and tweets to birds
unless I see the head-tip, open beak, and notes bursting
into the air. I can't learn a song unless I see the singer.

When I lose someone, I see them in half-glimpses
and shadows; a silhouette on a busy street,
a shape disappearing through a door, a chair
in shade, occupied until I turn my head.
How long must I hear a voice call as I fall asleep,
startle at the slant of a cheek glanced from a car,
wake to think someone just left the room.
I can't learn they've gone unless I see them leave.

Departures

For S.C.

There are times a long-dead person
comes up in conversation and no one knows
how or when they arrived; just a small moment's
breath to recognise their presence
before re-tellings of who they were,
how quick and brutal the illness,
or what they said that time around the fire.

We talk and the talk moves on
to other places, other people,
and maybe each of us has some unspoken
part pulled back in time.

The hospice on the last day
when each fought breath was counted,
when I saw how small the shape
under the sheets, how I knew
there would be no more paintings,
how you would no longer stretch
your dancer's body into Tai Chi forms,
how the poems you had still to write
would stretch with you into that greater space.

Suddenly, a frog

An X sliced corner to corner
allowed wet bark to spill, separate
into wedges, spread from a compact block
to a glistening heap.
The frog clambers up from the dark
chippings, piano-fingered hands spread to grip
bark as it shifts and slides, pauses on top
of the pile. I can see its throat pulsing, perfect
dots along sharp back-ridges, cleanly banded legs
in Halloween witch-stockings.
                    Suddenly, the taste of envy.
To slip into stasis, to lie still in darkness,
protected from unexpected upturning,
the resulting bumps and bruises. To not know
time passing and to emerge unsullied,
blinking at a new day, perfect.

Rooting Out

Tangles of roots baffle my fork's tines
as I push down into invaded earth,
each root twisting through clumps
of anchoring soil to clenching depth.
They snake to depths beyond my reach,
every knot pulled and shaken loose
leaves strands and fragments
of rhizomes to wait for space and rain,
sprout in neglected corners.

Mycelium nets under the grass,
through the woods, fibres feeding
on what has fallen, growing strong
in the rotting dark. There is no end,
no beginning, no centre to dig out,
only the evidence of bulbous clusters
swelling overnight in shady places.

It is too easy to rest, leave
a calm surface undisturbed, forget
what cells and spores lie beneath,
nursing malice as they spread.
Too easy to turn away from dark edges
and hard labour, ignore its silent seething,
until it shoots in all the overlooked quarters,
strong beyond all hope of rooting out
unless we can re-make the earth.

Wantwite likes company

tempts followers   flakes of pyrite   trails of
quartz   poisonous promises   gathers
panting crowds in its wake   they scrabble its
trail for gold-painted paper hearts   it throws
down   they clamber and kick   get close to
its breath   sweet miasma   shrinking ragged
hearts to flint

Desire Path

Fuse your fingers into blades to dig down
    into this path; mattock, hoe, spade,
whatever will scrape layers of packed earth
    down to footstep, root, and scuff.
Take a hazel stick for your spine, bend low
    to pick at prints made by heel
or toe, measure depths with your thumbnail,
    tallied with marks for past years.
You thought a desire line would run straight
    but follow the tracks as they sidestep
round obstacles or divert to smoother ground,
    eyes straining to see tread patterns
and foot size, peering to identify a man's boot,
    a woman's shoe. You want to know
whose need made this path you follow,
    and find that some prints are your own.

Strange Road

On this long road, on this bus,
how strange it is to accept
such changes; to be in one instant
at a work-day desk & in the next,
in this steel tube surrounded
by people I don't know, going to a city
I could so soon be lost in,
to be with people I've never met,
seeing unfamiliar trees from the windows.
Watching a plane hang in the sky
as it climbs from the airport,
yet another metal tube, and wondering
how it is we accept such impossibilities.
Such acceptance feels as strange
as the way wanting fades
when I can want something
so badly I can taste it; a coat
I don't need, a painting I have no space
for, a house that calls out to me
from its turrets and mullions.
Then in a day or two the wanting
is gone, dropped & un-remembered
like the way the cat comes in
with something small & furred
in his mouth, skulking through the door
as if someone may take his prize,
ready to growl & spit to defend it
but then drops it to call for food
or attention, uncaring of the scurry
under furniture, the escape
to a dark corner.

Blame

She looks outside, twenty-eight days with no rain
and the grass is browning to the colour of barley
while she cruises online for someone to blame.
She tweets and follows women who arrange
campaigns and marches to call out patriarchy
while outside it is now thirty-five days with no rain.
Buttons to click, petitions to sign for refugees' pain,
shared outrage when protests are met with army
bullets, she types long posts about who to blame
and rages at answers that seem to mansplain.
She reads manifestos for a pure-enough party
to care about fifty-nine days with no rain.
Another jerk shouts *All Lives Matter* again
and Sparrow wonders who has time for the malarkey
of searching all day for someone to blame.
She's tired, this level of anger can't be sustained
Sparrow says it won't matter, come the terminarchy;
outside it's been a hundred days without rain
and spending all day online is partly to blame.

Second Wind

There are secrets, well kept,
about what may bloom in barren lands:
Buddleia always finds a place to root
in concrete, rubble, abandoned spaces
and the sculptor's favourite chisel
is the one worn to the shape of his hand
through years of coaxing art from stone.

There are consolations in stiffening joints
slowing my walks on the limestone hills:
the way a violet nestles in a knuckle of root
or the questing eye-stalk of a Roman snail
snaps into focus. Years sprint by, spill
duties and obligations to lie by the wayside
leave days that stretch into space
for new passions or old obsessions.

There are secrets, better kept,
about what may slip past fences
as wild garlic grows where it will,
stretches past boundaries and barriers,
indifferent to the effect of its scent
on senses, or whether you admire
its pale blooms' constellations.

Fallow

Nothing happens in the between times, emptiness
seeps through TV screens, slips under silent doors, pools
on quiet pavements where fliers for sales and shows
tangle in hedge-roots and tatter into gutters.
The sky is pale and damp, uncertain
between clear and cloud, and a few limp leaves
cling to dark branches. The year holds a breath
while the clock ticks and the afternoon fades.
Quietness eases through the house and outside
small birds chirp in the hedge, settle to rest.

Down Piggy Lane

The path skulks round the back end of a housing estate,
hidden by overgrown shrubs and tattered trees
either side of the sullen brook. Scraps and patches
of land line the trail, once-proud fences sagging between.
Pig arks are empty, fading grass straggling
up the sides. Competing cockerels shout
from pens, hidden by a clutter of buckets,
upturned feed tubs and a green-scummed bath.

Every patch has a shed or shelter, all alike
in their difference. Walls patched
with multi-coloured iron, rust collecting
in the corrugations. Here an old front door
with a fanlight and ghost of a number,
there the lichened side of a caravan.

My foot catches in the muddy ruts and humps
of the path and I stumble into a memory
of dreaming through afternoon school,
waiting for when nine-year-old legs could pump
the bike pedals, carrying a Tupperware beaker
of milk for feral kittens and windfall apples
stuffed under my jumper for a shaggy piebald pony.

How have I forgotten all I wanted then?
To own one of those fields, to live
in a ramshackle shed with the kittens
and the pony's head looking through
feed-sack curtains, a few large dogs,
a nest of slow worms under the floor
and any other creature who found me.
How once such things were enough.

Getting Late

Four in the afternoon and the mist is rising
from the field, snagging on tufted humps
of yellowed grass, blurring the path.
Across the stream, sounds rise
from the playing field hidden
by willow and a tangle of brambles.

A whoop and rumble of boys' voices
from the bike track counterpoints
the tinny rhythm of their phones
on Spotify and the higher squeals
from smaller children seem to float
across the space, confound distance.

A new build looms behind the boundary,
square-cornered and blank-eyed
while the sky dissolves into pastel
stripes behind the sharp roof-ridge
and small birds chunter their bedtime
calls in the trees and hedges.

The oak is bare of leaves and squirrels,
acorns all taken or sunk into the mud.
Rooks gather, their rusty calls ratcheting
from the branches and a voice whispers
at my shoulder *Nice place, if you can keep it.*

Lightfall

There is a light may fall as a year turns,
kinder than summer's unforgiving light
which scours corners and searchlights
faults. A light which glimmers behind
a row of leaf-stripped willow and fires
late-to-fall leaves to gold. A light to draw
long shade over dew-damp fields
and shine grass webs to billowing silver.
A light which fades quickly and kindly,
making way for a fire-lit night.

Missing the Blood Moon

I didn't stay up to make noise,
didn't clash and rattle pots and pans
or set the dogs to howl, didn't shout
at the sky as the moon bled. I slept

under its light as it strained through
curtains and blinds, unconcerned
about end-times, keeping my head
covered, or curling my fingers
into fists to guard any temptation
of pointing. I know the morning

will bring scrolls of photographs
some filling the screen
and detailed in red-washed craters,
others pale and far-off
like a hole-punch scrap.
All seen through a lens as if reality and risk
can no longer be judged by eyes alone.

Wantwite needs slaves

Draws them in   spells and sigils   offers food   shelter
calls them   under flowing robes   support   heft
of feet   it blinds   acid drips of reward   heaps slab-
weight on shoulders   necks bend   backs break
muscle and bone   wear down   to dust   makes
pathway   Wantwite's feet pound

How to be alone

Begin with wood. Maybe a log left from tree-cutting,
not pine but something with weight, something
that fits the curve of one arm, cradling. A measure
from heel to knee, bark willing to slough under a chisel.

Take your time with hollowing; feel the log's resistance
between your knees, the chisel's handle wearing
into your palm. It will give up its heart to you,
one pale sliver after another, to feed the fire.

Measure the hollow with your hands; drip linseed
into its wounds, watch the stripped flesh darken as it drinks.
Its outside will challenge, teach your hands to ache,
to show what blossoms while you sandpaper every snag.

It's going too far to start with the goat; the messy business
of skinning and scraping can be done by those who need to.
Buy rawhide. Leave it to soak, watch how water cajoles it
to softness while you smooth and polish, oil and smooth.

When you have polished the wood for a day and a night,
the skin will be supple and ready to offer to the drum.
Lace it slowly, turning it round between your thighs,
tightening each line until the lace whitens your fingers.

As the skin dries and hums with tension, be gentle.
A finger stroke is enough to hear it finding a voice;
it will sing for you when it's ready.

Muscle Memory

These hands have others' habits ingrained,
set deep into the lines on my palms.
I hold my hand up to the sun
or a bright lamp, see genetics glowing
through my fingers, pulsing in my veins.

The lift of kettle, cup, the snug of peeler
against my thumb, the stretch of fingers
around a winter potato. How to tong coal
on to a new fire or draw the flame
with newspaper held tight across the grate.
My hands remember how to rock a crying infant,
how to wipe a child's face, the *O* of her mouth
disappearing like a moon behind cloud.

New habits have rooted into muscle and sinew;
eyeing a spirit level, marking a wall,
how to hold a hammer drill so it doesn't skip
away from the mark. How to cut a mitre,
chisel a mortice, wire a plug, or bend electronic
memory, keyboard and screen to my intention.
These hands remember how to drip wax for batik,
how to cut a stencil or mould soft clay.

Some habits wash away like the day's grime,
The weight of hymn book, the shape of prayer,
the smoothing of white gloves at Easter
or the wriggle of the side zip on a new dress.
These fingers have never learned the habit
of knitting or crochet, have long forgotten
the weight and dent of a wedding ring.

Grave

I browse in the stonemason's yard,
cup the palm of my hand over the curve
of an angel's wing, the smooth bulb of an urn.
I trace my finger along the sharp valleys
of newly-chiselled *Rest in Peace* and *Much Loved*
Wife and Mother. I watch my shifting
reflection in black marble, crouch to hold
a cold cherub in my arms, but tell
the suited salesman that I'm just looking.

My bones won't rest in the ground.
Humerus and femur will hollow into wind chimes,
wrist and ankle bones make rattles for dark nights,
and the cap of my skull will catch light
on a windowsill, on a hill.

Conversion

The little gods of the geriatric hospital are lost;
they miss the soft shuffle of slippered feet
and the mumbles of confusion. They hunch
in the corners, not knowing how to ease
a last breath or soothe anxious muttering
for the loud men in hard hats who block
old wards with new walls and divert long
corridors into angles and dead ends.

They watch the machinery, the scaffolding,
bewildered by signs that talk of *lifestyle*
and *show apartment*. They filch glossy paper
and puzzle over *retirement in mind*.
They know Matron would scowl
at the dust-trapping draperies and can't see
where the sluice is hidden in the shiny white
cupboards. They retreat to the attics and wait;
time will bring them work to do.

Wantwite is sickening

Rotting   ulcerated skin blisters   peels raggedy strips
tangles followers   fetid spatter   suits   shoes   scar
faces   seal eyes   wantwite won't stop   won't fall
held up   gold-soaked bones   silver marrow   tracks
hiss spit caustic steam   path cratered   earth wounded

Nearly

Those times I dreamt of falling,
legs pedalling air, arms akimbo,
no knowledge of where the fall began
or where it will end. All the times
a scream pummelled inside my ribs,
stuck in my throat, stretched my mouth
to silence so that accelerating air
could howl in my ears and ripple my skin.
And the times I spasmed awake, a gasp
loud in the dark room, remembering
those warnings *if you hit the ground*
before you wake, you'll die.
And thinking of those times, driving
on a fast road where maybe five minutes
later a lorry blows a tyre and hits a car
or times I swallow and don't choke
or times I stumble and recover
and don't hit my head, don't lie
in a bed with lights bleeping
and machines inflating my chest,
faking my breath.
              I don't know now
if it's better to know about nearly,
if it's better to live oblivious,
or let *nearly* jolt us awake, each time.

Sparrow says

leave the hedgerow for the birds,
there's little to learn
from what's been tamed
and trimmed to fit a space.
Sparrow's fury torchlights the way
to wilder places where pleasantries
won't cut thorny tangles and smiles
don't lighten shadows. Sparrow leads
past trodden paths, turns away
from easy trails, breaks through canopies
with whoops and yells of rebellion.

Sparrow chuckles
        from the armchair, leans
        against the door post,
        waits on every path or way.
He nudges at my back, finger-prods my ribs,
hovers at my shoulder, tells me to speak up,
stand up, don't hide behind doors or screens.
Sparrow pulls me to the sea, the moor,
the forest; his boot slams on his spade's lug
and he digs. He shows me no-one can mend
fractured land, no-one can re-plant ancient.

Wild Seed

A song playing on the radio starts the dog
howling. He lifts his muzzle to the ceiling and makes
that shape with his mouth you see no other time
as if only the sustained *baroo* of his howl can speak
to whatever-it-is, what tone, what note, can reach
deep into his core and pull out this ancestral cry.

You laugh and the dog wags his tail as he howls
but amusement only disguises the itch inside, to know
what he hears, what old demand draws this from him,
what longing. You want to feel it; the imperative
bred in the bone, blood-seeded. You want to be driven

to run through the woods uncaring of hawthorn's rip
or nettle's sting; you want to grow old and mad,
to scare children with your nocturnal walks
and sly curses. You want to be anti-social,
to answer an irresistible demand to squat naked
on the grass and straighten your open throat,
to throw a wordless challenge to the distance.

Endlings

drift over the earth, gather
in loose clusters, their calls echo
then cease.

Predators ignore their prey, run together,
scan and scent the ground on hill and heath
in widening circles until resigned, they lie down
alone.
   The Thylacine doesn't try; he's released
both need and drive, has given up and found
a place to lie still as he blurs and fades
to become just a shadow
on the ground.

On a branch above,
the passenger pigeon waits;
her claws no longer able to uncurl,
tree-bark patterning feathers as if braided
in mist. Tattered butterflies whirl
between leaves; don't settle or rest,
passed over by birds. The Laughing Owl,
the Forest Thrush, circle the sky
possessed
by an older, greater need and scarred
by hope, until exhaustion brings peace
in death.
A Barbary lion calls in the hills, unmarked
and Sparrow weeps for the want of an ark.

Living Yule

I was there, when men squatted on haunches
to chip flint and weave webs of belief from seasons
and circles of death and growth.
The stink of boar-grease stiffening my braid
and blue whorls whispering under my skin
offered hope that darkness could end.

I put on homespun robes and tonsured my head
to walk the years when dogma stalked faith;
smoothing old ways and old faces to new shapes,
nudging builders to find safe spaces in stone arches.
Heedless of changed names for the turns of the year,
I watched the ploughman bury cakes for first cut,
crooned the song of seasons round to seed-time.

I've paced the years' life and I am still here to die
ever again. Hide me beneath plastic and tinsel,
dress me in red, fatten my cheeks, sweeten my story;
the scent of old circles clings to the shade of man.

Notes and Acknowledgements

Note on titles: The word 'endling' means the last of any species. For a long time, this collection was going to be titled *Endling* but that title had been taken elsewhere. The other word for the last of a species is 'terminarch'. Adding a 'y' softened the sound and suggested a different direction; we are used to talking about patriarchy, monarchy, oligarchy, perhaps we should think about whether we are heading for terminarchy.

Versions of some of these poems have appeared in *The Phare, One Hand Clapping, The Interpreter's House, Atrium, Under the Radar, The Honest Ulsterman, Prole, London Grip,* and *The Stony Thursday Book.*